Annie Oakley

A Captivating Guide to an American Sharpshooter Who Later Became a Wild West Folk Hero

Free Bonus from Captivating History
(Available for a Limited time)

Hi History Lovers!

Now you have a chance to join our exclusive history list so you can get your first history ebook for free as well as discounts and a potential to get more history books for free! Simply visit the link below to join.

Captivatinghistory.com/ebook

Also, make sure to follow us on Facebook, Twitter and Youtube by searching for Captivating History.

Contents

Introduction

How could Annie Oakley, a woman of barely 110 pounds, beat so many of the greatest sharpshooters with her skill and talent?

The name is probably familiar to most readers, but not many know about her early life or her great love for her husband, who was also a sharpshooter. We are taking you back more than a century to meet one of the greatest American folklore heroines who ever existed. Annie Oakley dazzled and awed millions of people during her career and met some of the most memorable people of her time, including Thomas Edison, Sitting Bull, Prince Edward, and the queen of England herself.

Annie Oakley is just one of the many impressive legends of the Wild West, and her journey took her from the small town of Greenville in Darke County, Ohio, to some of the biggest stages in America and Europe.

Embark on that journey with Annie Oakley, from her humble beginnings to the glory and fame she achieved as one of the greatest sharpshooters of the Wild West, where legends of cowboys and sharpshooters abounded as one of the greatest nations of today was being forged.

Chapter 1 –Phoebe Ann Moses: Early Life of Miss Sharpshooter

Before Annie Oakley became known as "Little Miss Sure Shot" and one of the greatest Wild West heroes, she was known by her birth name: Phoebe Ann Moses.

Phoebe Ann Moses was born on August 13th, 1860, around two miles northwest of Woodland, now known as the small unincorporated community of Willowdell in Darke County, Ohio. The county got its name after William Darke, who was an officer in the American Revolutionary War. Darke County was peaceful farmland, and it had been mostly inhabited by Native Americans until they lost the Battle of Fallen Timbers to General "Mad" Anthony Wayne in 1794. After the battle, settlers started flocking in. The battle was symbolically named, as the area of Darke County was covered in lush, thick virgin forests that seemed to have no end; at least, that was the case before the battle against the confederation of Native American tribes took place. Once the battle was won, the settlers cleared the forest and started cultivating corn.

Annie's father, Jacob Moses, fought in the War of 1812, which was a conflict between the United States and the United Kingdom, although both sides had assistance, mainly from the Native

Americans. The war ended in February 1815 after a peace treaty. A little over thirty years later, in 1848, Annie's parents, Susan Wise and Jacob Moses, would get married. Annie's mother was eighteen, while Jacob was close to turning fifty.

Around 1855, the Moses family decided to take a chance and moved west to Darke County, Ohio, where they rented a farm. At this point, the family consisted of Susan, Jacob, and their five young daughters (Mary Jane, Lydia, Elizabeth, Sarah Ellen, and Catherine). Jacob Moses also brought along his Kentucky rifle, which can only be described as an extension of his own body, as he was rather skillful in hunting and shooting. Jacob Moses, who was an athletic man despite being in his late fifties, was ready for a life of hard work in a new settlement.

When the family first arrived in Darke County, it was rather rural, as it had no railway service or even a general store. The Moses family lived in a cabin along the borders of the state of Indiana, five miles east of North Star. Jacob built the family cabin out of timber, and Annie would be born there only five years later.

Annie was Susan and Jacob's sixth child out of the nine they had together. Besides her five sisters, who were mentioned above, the Moses family would later grow to include John and Hulda. Susan and Jacob had more children, but they did not survive past infancy.

Susan Wise was the one who decided to name her baby Phoebe Ann; however, Phoebe's sisters started calling her Annie, so her given name didn't stick for long. Annie was a small girl with dark hair and bright blue eyes. She was strong for her size and had a direct gaze that caught people's attention.

While Annie had many sisters to play and spend time with, she wasn't that interested in playing with them. Instead of dressing up dolls, Annie enjoyed tagging along with her father, who frequently hunted and set traps in the woods to provide food for his big family. The little curious Annie enjoyed learning more about hunting and trapping from her father, who unknowingly prepared his young daughter to take over his role as the family's caretaker. Annie's only surviving brother was one year younger, which might be why her father decided to teach Annie what he knew about hunting, weapons, and trapping. Still, even though her brother John was a year younger, he also tagged along with his father and sister when their father went hunting, as well as when they worked around the farm. They built fences, butchered cows, collected and cultivated apples, beans, and corn, and gathered berries and nuts from the forest. Even though Annie assisted her father with his work around the farm, she found marksmanship the most interesting of all. Annie was fascinated with guns and hunting from an early age. Her father taught her the ways of the forest surrounding their rough cabin, teaching her how to make traps out of cornstalk and track rabbits, which she would bring home as family dinner. Annie was a true tomboy and a rather vivacious little girl.

When she was only six years old, Annie's father died, and the family faced hard times. Jacob Moses got hypothermia in 1865 during a blizzard, after which he became an invalid, struggling to provide for his family due to his illness. He died from pneumonia in 1866, leaving Susan widowed and alone with their eight children. Annie's life and carefree childhood would change from that point on.

After her father died, Annie couldn't attend school regularly, although she would later go back to school in her later childhood and adulthood. The family was also forced to move to a smaller home in Darke County. However, her interest in guns, hunting, and marksmanship didn't die with her father. Annie became rather skillful at trapping before the age of seven, and she would be the one to bring meat to the table and feed her family.

Annie was only eight years old the first time she tried to shoot a gun, and she didn't just "try"—she excelled. It was her first move toward becoming one of the best shooters the Wild West ever saw. As she recalled later, she used her father's old muzzle-loading rifle for her first kill shot. Since her father was dead, his Kentucky rifle hung above the fireplace. Annie was not allowed to take the rifle, even though her father had taught her the basics of shooting before his death. Despite the rule imposed by her mother, Annie took the rifle regardless. She managed to shoot a squirrel off the fence of her family's backyard by steadying the gun on the porch rails, and her mother preserved the meat. That was only the beginning of Annie's contribution to her family. Even though Annie used the rifle to help feed her poor family, her mother was utterly upset with seeing one of her youngest children, a girl at that, using a firearm.

One of the historians who wrote about the history of Darke County, Frazer Wilson, claims that Annie's brother was angry that his sister had a chance to shoot a rifle. Wilson writes that her brother John was so agitated that he decided to double the load for his gun. He handed the gun to Annie afterward, believing that the kick would be so strong that it would discourage her from shooting a gun ever again. However, it seems that marksmanship was in Annie's blood. John wanted to use his hat as a target, and he tossed the hat up in the air. According to Frazer Wilson, Annie's shot was so smooth and quick that it promptly made a clean hole in her brother's hat. It was not a common thing for a girl to shoot a gun, and a girl so talented in marksmanship was an even rarer thing to see in that period.

By the age of eight, Annie was hunting and trapping, not only to place food on the family's table but also to sell. She sold the game in Greenville to people such as shopkeepers G. Anthony and Charles Katzenberger. The game she sold would then be resold and shipped to hotels in Cincinnati and other cities. Her mother insisted that Annie go back to school and stop using a rifle, as she was scared of having one of her youngest children, a girl at that, shooting guns with no real supervision. Still, Annie remained a fruitful provider in her family.

In 1867, Annie's sister, Mary Jane, died of tuberculosis, and her widowed mother had to sell their family cow named "Pink" to pay for the medical and funeral bills. Soon afterward, since food was scarce and Susan was only earning $1.25 per week, she gave her youngest daughter, Hulda, to the wealthy Bartholomew family, who watched over Hulda for a short period of time until Susan could get back on her feet.

In 1870, Annie and her sister, Sarah Ellen, were sent to the Darke County Infirmary, as the family was struggling to survive. In the spring of the same year, Annie was sent to a local farmer, where she was supposed to get an education and help with their infant son, for which she was supposed to be compensated 50 cents per week. The payment turned out to be nothing more than a false promise, as the family essentially made Annie a slave. She was expected to do all the hard work around the farm for free, and she did not receive any kind of education. Annie spoke about her experience working on that farm later in life, saying she was "a prisoner" and the family were "wolves." She describes the farmer as a "wolf in sheep's clothing," but she never revealed their true names.

Annie's work on the farm would have been exhausting even if she was a man, as she had to get up before everyone, milk the cows, skim the milk, make breakfast, wash the dishes, work around the garden and farm, feed the farm animals, put the farmer's baby to sleep, pump the water for the cattle, pick wild berries, and make dinner. Annie recalled that her mother sent her letters, telling her to come back home, but they wouldn't let her. They wrote letters back to her mother, saying she was happy and content.

Annie also recalled that she was physically abused, mentioning scars on her back, probably from whippings, although she never revealed the extent to which she was abused during her time on that farm. She did disclose that the farmer's wife threw her out barefoot in the snow after she had accidentally fallen asleep during her work. Annie would have died from cold if the farmer hadn't let her back into the house. In 1872, Annie decided she was done with the "wolves" and ran away.

A kindly man paid her train fare, and she returned to the infirmary and discovered there was a new superintendent in charge, Samuel Crawford Edington, who lived there with his wife Nancy and their children. Unlike the former superintendent, who had sent Annie right into a den of wolves, Edington and his wife made friends with Annie and treated her as their child. Annie later said later that Nancy was a friend of her mother's, which might have been why the Edington family accepted Annie as one of their own.

Annie was invited to live and sleep in the living quarters of the infirmary, and the couple taught her embroidery, sewing, and the art of decorating. They also paid Annie for her efforts, as Annie sewed orphans' uniforms, dresses, and quilts. She even learned how to make lovely cuffs and collars that made the dark uniforms seem brighter. Annie became close to the Edington children, with whom she attended school. The family placed their faith and trust in Annie, and although she was only a young girl, Samuel Edington put her in charge of the infirmary's dairy. The infirmary had twelve cows, and she would milk all of them, then proceed to collect the cream, out of which she made butter. Soon, Annie got a raise and started to save some money.

Annie spent around three years with the Edingtons, and when she was about fifteen years old, she decided to return home to her mother. At the time, her mother had already remarried and was building a house near the crossroads at North Star. On her return, Annie decided to stop by the store that belonged to the Katzenberger brothers, where she used to sell the game she hunted and trapped. She offered to bring game to the Katzenberger brothers, who would then sell it to hotels, in return for compensation that would help her earn a living and escape poverty. The Katzenbergers accepted her offer, and Annie would spend the rest of her life making a living with her marksmanship and trapping skills.

Annie made a great business deal and had major plans for her future. Despite the hardships she had endured, including her father's and sister's death and the experiences with the "wolves," Annie stood proud and was determined to make her dreams come true.

Chapter 2 – The Huntress of the North Star

Annie decided to escape poverty by relying on what she did best—shooting, trapping, and hunting. Unlike many hunters, who preferred shooting their game when their target was still, Annie always shot moving targets. She wrote in her autobiography that it is only fair to give the animal you are hunting a fair chance to escape or dodge the shot. Her shot, however, couldn't be dodged. Annie appeared to be born to hold a gun in her hand, and whatever the target was, she would shoot right through it. Her aim was flawless, and her hand was steady, so even when the game was in motion, she could make a kill shot, which made her an exceptional hunter.

However, this took practice, and in the beginning, she was determined to improve her hunting skills as much as she could. She started hunting small game, such as rabbits and quail, and learned where the game would hide. In her autobiography, Annie talked about how easy it was for her to track game and make exceptional shots, which made her business with the Katzenberger brothers flourish. Annie said, "Nothing more simple, I assure you. But I'll tell you what. You must have your mind, and nerve, and everything in harmony. Don't look at your gun, simply follow the object with the end of it, as if the tip of the barrel was the point of your finger."

Like her father before her, Annie's gun was an extension of her body. Annie was the happiest girl in the world when she smelled the scent of burnt gunpowder, and she was at her most natural when she was alone in the wilderness and on the hunt. She hunted all her game fairly, allowing the animals to be on the move and giving her targets a chance to escape the destiny that would be served by her steady hand. The way Annie hunted, with the game on the move, made her an even better shooter, as she had to learn how to be quick with her trigger finger and her eye.

The Katzenberger brothers grew fond of Annie. It is no real surprise why. Besides delivering an abundance of game to the brothers, Annie was also very likable, although perhaps a bit odd. They decided to send Annie a special gift, and on one Christmas, Annie was given two boxes of percussion caps, one can of DuPont Eagle ducking black powder, and five pounds of shot. The powder she received was of the highest quality on the market, and Annie was so enchanted with her new gift that she couldn't bring herself to open the can for days. Soon afterward, Annie received another gift, a gift that would change her marksmanship game for the better. This present was a Parker Brothers 16-gauge breech-loading hammer with one hundred brass shells. Other girls would be thrilled to get a new dress or a piece of jewelry, but Annie's perfect present was a shotgun that showcased the power of innovation in the world of firearms. Breech-loading guns appeared in the United States around the late 1870s, and they were far more efficient than the previous generation of muzzle-loading rifles, which could fail a shooter if the powder got wet. Shooters also didn't have to bring a powder horn and a ramrod with them, making shooting and hunting more efficient. Now, Annie could just load the gun shells with powder before hunting and simply insert them in the barrel while she was out looking for game.

Not only was Annie's new gun more convenient to use, but it also allowed her to hunt more game. She started sending game in batches of six or a dozen to the Katzenberger store, from where it would be sent to hotels and restaurants from Greenville to Cincinnati and the surrounding area. There is a legend that the restaurant and hotel guests preferred the game shot by Annie, as she would make a kill shot through the head. However, as is the case with many other Wild West figures, there is no way to confirm if this was true or only a folk story.

At the time, there were no limitations when it came to the number of wild animals that could be hunted, as the preservation of wildlife wasn't of great concern to the settlers in the United States. That meant a successful hunter could hunt as much as he or she wanted, allowing them to make a substantial amount of money in the process. If one truly worked at it, hunters could make a higher yearly profit than a miner, lumberjack, or an average farmer. Still, a huntress was a rare thing, which was why Annie came across as an odd girl to many, although everyone was fascinated by her marksmanship skills. She was well known in all of North Star and the wider area by the time she was sixteen.

Annie Oakley by Baker's Art Gallery, c. 1880.

Working as a market hunter, Annie paid off her mother's mortgage in less than a year. Annie was a determined and hard-working girl, and she was proud of herself for being self-sufficient. Annie was so proud of her earning power that she used to say with great pleasure that ever since she was ten years old, she didn't have a dollar that she hadn't earned herself.

Before Annie was in her late teens, she had won so many shooting contests that she was banned from entering any more. She had also shot so much game that she was embarrassed to see her total kill number in the Katzenberger's books once limitations were brought about to regulate hunters and the number of animals they could kill in a season.

Everyone in North Star and Darke County knew Annie by her reputation. However, her life was about to change yet again, this time right on the doorstep of early adulthood.

Chapter 3 – Annie and the Star Shooters of the West

Annie must have been an odd sight to see back in the day. She wore long stockings made of yarn, boots with copper toes, a short dress with knickerbockers, and mittens with a stitched-in trigger finger. Annie compensated for her oddities with her marksmanship skills and hunting talent. However, Annie wasn't the only exceptional shooter that America talked about.

The name of Captain Adam H. Bogardus appears in the annals of leading sharpshooters in 1869, which was the year when Bogardus became famous for shooting a hundred pigeons without missing a single target. The same year, Bogardus made a bet with Mr. R. M. Patchen that he could shoot and kill 500 pigeons in 645 minutes. Not only did Bogardus succeed in shooting all 500 pigeons, but he also managed to do so in 528 minutes. By the time Annie was fifteen, Bogardus had become the national trap shooter champion after defeating Ira Paine. After becoming a champion in the United States, Bogardus traveled to England, where he challenged anyone who wanted to compete against him in shooting. He won eighteen matches, which brought him distinction as a world trap shooter champion.

In the 1870s and 1880s, there were plenty of champion shooters, and the number of exhibition shooters was increasing as well. Bogardus was only one such champion, with William Frank "Doc" Carver being his greatest rival. One day in 1878, Doc dressed up, wearing a velvet shirt and a large sombrero with his pants tucked in his long boots. He made his way to Deerfoot Park in New York City with an ambitious plan—he was going to shoot and break 5,500 glass balls in 500 minutes with his Winchester rifle, a shooting stunt that had never been done with a rifle. Doc's assistant tossed the glass balls, which were filled with white feathers, and as they were thrown into the air, Doc would shoot each one. Some park visitors left Deerfoot Park, as the noise of the gun being fired was too loud and frequent, but many stayed to watch the show, which started at 11 o'clock sharp.

Whenever Doc would empty one gun, another freshly loaded and oiled gun would be handed to him, and the used gun would be placed in a barrel of water so it could cool down. The sulfur, broken glass, smoke, dirty water, and feathers made Doc's eyes become inflamed, and it got to the point that he had to pause and place a handkerchief filled with ice on his eyes to get some relief. Once he felt he couldn't go on any longer, he found out that he only had eighteen minutes left to shoot one hundred feather-filled glass balls. He made it to his goal with ten minutes to spare. Even though he succeeded, Doc spent the most painful night of his life in his bed with his eyes aching so much that he said he would never do such a thing again.

Exhibition shooting was a rather competitive sport, and shooters were always trying to outperform one another. Annie wasn't the first woman to join this sport, which considered to be more appropriate for men. John Ruth's wife also enjoyed partaking in shooting shows with her husband in Deerfoot Park. Mrs. Ruth would use a mirror and shoot with her back turned to the target, and she would also shoot glass balls her husband tossed—her aim was incredible, as she rarely missed. John Ruth wasn't a bad shooter either. However, none of them were nearly as famous as Captain Bogardus or Doc Walker.

Exhibition shooters had performed with circuses and other traveling shows since the early 1800s, but it reached its peak in the 1880s. It became so popular that even a twelve-year-old girl claimed to be the champion of the world, holding a $500 bet that she could shoot and break 1,000 glass balls in 50 minutes.

One of the famous exhibition shooters that used to perform with theatrical troops and organized shows was Frank E. Butler. Butler arrived in America as an Irish immigrant. He was below average in height for a man, but he was attractive and had a good sense of humor. Butler liked to tell stories to make people laugh, and he worked on any job he could get upon arriving in the United States. Before he became an exhibition shooter, Butler trained dogs for a theatrical troop. He wasn't brilliant in this endeavor, but better times were ahead, as Butler decided to start practicing shooting. He trained himself by shooting at a target bent backward while holding a mirror. Butler found a partner in Baughman, and they performed with a poodle they called George in various New York City theaters in 1875. Around 1881, Butler and Baughman decided to join the Sells Brothers Circus. The Sells brothers—Allen, Peter, Lewis, and Ephraim—were the head of one of the leading entertainment attractions. They had over ten years of experience in the industry and billed their entertainment business as "The Biggest Amusement Enterprise on Earth." Joining the Sells brothers was a good choice for the pair, as Butler and Baughman performed in numerous acts and shows all across the United States, which gave them a regular income.

When they were welcomed to the Sells brothers' business, Baughman and Butler were told to pack their bags and leave the hotel in Cincinnati where they were staying and come to Columbus, Ohio, where the new season for the circus was about to start at the end of April 1881.

In the hotel where they were staying, Butler was asked by one of the farmers who frequented the hotel about what he could do with his gun and if he could shoot a little, offering a hundred dollar bet if he could beat a local legend. What Butler didn't know was that he would be competing against Annie Oakley. Butler accepted the challenge, which required him to travel from Cincinnati to Greenville. Since the journey to Greenville wasn't too long and since he needed the money, Butler decided to go before leaving for Columbus with his partner. Butler most likely thought it would be easy money, as he thought he could outshoot any shooter except for the likes of Bogardus and Doc.

After reaching Greenville, Butler had to make his way to a little town known as North Star. He still didn't know who his opponent was. The townsfolk would only tell him that he would measure his skill against their local sharpshooter.

Frank E. Butler, Courtesy by the Annie Oakley Center at Garst Museum

https://commons.wikimedia.org/wiki/File:Frank_E_Butler_c1882.png

Once he arrived at North Star, Frank Butler was presented with his opponent, and he couldn't have been more surprised to see a slim, short girl, wearing a short linsey dress and knickerbockers, as she readied herself to shoot the moving targets prepared for the occasion.

Butler often spoke about his first encounter with Annie, doing so on at least three different occasions in 1903 and twice in 1924. Butler told reporters that nothing could have prepared him for the surprise he encountered in North Star. He was caught off guard, describing the outcome as Annie's first big match and his first defeat. On that day, Annie shot twenty-three birds, while Butler killed twenty-one.

At the time, Annie was in her early twenties, and she was quite a sight to behold, with her long dark hair and piercing blue eyes. After the match was over, Frank invited Annie to see his act that he performed with his poodle George. Annie accepted his invitation and was thrilled with Butler's poodle. Frank showed her some of his acts, such as shooting an apple placed on the poodle's head. The poodle would sit still, which allowed Butler to shoot the apple easily, making it burst into pieces.

When Annie came to see the act, Butler picked up a piece of the apple he shot and placed it by Annie's boot. This is how the romance between the shooting pair commenced. Annie was shy and reluctant when it came to courting, and even if she had any suitors other than Frank Butler, she never talked about them. George was somewhat an intermediary in their romantic relationship. Even though she was already twenty-one, to Frank, Annie seemed like a little girl, while to Annie, Frank must have seemed like a worldly man.

When Frank left for Columbus to join the Sells Brothers Circus, they kept in touch. Frank would send her greetings and presents in the name of George, his poodle.

Frank was a man of many talents, and one of these talents was writing poetry. He frequently sent letters to Annie, one of which included the poem that was inspired by his love for Annie. Frank called the poem "Little Raindrops."

There's a charming little girl
She's many miles from here
She's a loving little fairy
You'd fall in love to see her
Her presence would remind you

Of an angel in the skies,

And you bet I love this little girl

With the raindrops in her eyes.

Frank was married before he arrived in the United States, having two children with his first wife. Their marriage took a wrong turn, although Frank was a good man who never drank, gambled, or had problems with the law.

Things get a little muddy when it comes to the date of Frank and Annie's marriage. Not even their closest relatives knew the exact date. It is believed the pair married on June 20th, 1882, in Ontario, Canada. This book places the initial meeting of Frank and Annie in 1881, but some scholars place the famous shooting contest as taking place in 1875. If this is true, their marriage would have taken place in 1876. It is possible the contradictory dates have to do with Butler's divorce from his first wife, which was finalized in 1876. Whatever the case may be, they married a year after they met, meaning Annie was either sixteen or twenty-two when she married Frank. If she was sixteen, it is also possible that the couple decided to keep the exact date of their wedding a secret, as Annie left Darke Country before the wedding, which wasn't proper behavior for an unmarried girl back then.

According to some sources, after their marriage, Frank sent Annie to a Catholic school in Erie, Pennsylvania. While Frank traveled with the Sells Brothers Circus, Annie stayed there and received additional education. However, it is not known for sure if this actually happened. If it did, Frank completed the contract he had with the Sells brothers and found himself a new partner, John Graham, while Annie finished up her schooling.

It is known that Graham's mother was the head of a boarding school in Erie, and it has been recorded that Butler was a visitor there at the time when Annie was residing in Erie. It is suggested that Annie might have stayed with Graham's mother at the time, as the story of Annie attending a Catholic school is not confirmed by any written records.

Graham and Butler created quite a name for themselves while touring the United States, calling themselves "America's all rifle team and champion shot" and awing people who attended their shows with shooting stunts. The pair shot apples off each other's heads, and Butler also shot targets bent backward while holding a rifle upside down between his knees.

In 1882, while Graham and Butler were performing in Ohio, the name Annie Oakley wasn't on everyone's lips, but that was about to change. Soon after, Annie left Erie and joined her husband, and soon, all of America knew the name of Annie Oakley.

Chapter 4 – The Birth of Annie Oakley

Soon after leaving Erie, Phoebe Ann Moses would become known as Annie Oakley, one of America's most treasured folklore heroes.

Annie left Erie either at the end of 1882 or the beginning of 1883 to join her husband. Even when Annie joined Butler, who was working with Graham at the time, she didn't join the duo as a shooter. According to Annie's autobiography, she would never have become a part of Butler's act if Graham hadn't become ill before one of their shooting shows. Since he was left without a partner and had an audience waiting to be amused with some exhibition target shooting, Butler asked Annie to hold objects that he would then shoot.

Annie agreed, and she became a part of the show, but she did not shoot until one particular day. Butler used to amuse his audience by missing a couple of his targets on purpose at the beginning of a show. That way, he could stun his audience once he started shooting targets without missing. One day while Annie was assisting him, Butler kept missing his targets to the point where the audience started to disapprove. According to Butler, who later spoke about the event, a man from the audience stood up and demanded Butler to let the girl,

Annie, shoot the target instead, as he had missed the target over a dozen times.

Annie obliged and took the gun. She had never practiced on the targets Butler used for the show, but she still managed to hit the target on her second try. The audience was thrilled and cheered for Annie to continue. She never missed a single target from that point on. As Butler recalled, he tried to resume his act and take the gun back from Annie, but he was howled down and had to let Annie finish the act. Butler knew better than to let Annie go back into the shadows, so he suggested she become a regular part of the act. Annie would become the star of the show, even though Butler's name preceded hers in the show's announcement. The two never competed against each other from that point on. As Frank Butler liked to say, Annie outclassed him in what he did best, which was shooting targets and putting on a show for his audience.

Frank Butler decided to teach Annie everything he knew about sharpshooting show business and allowed her to have the spotlight. As mentioned above, Annie wasn't the only girl competing for fame in the world of sharpshooting, as there was a great number of women who performed for audiences as sharpshooters. Tillie Russell and Lillian Smith were just some of many women seeking to become famous, but unlike those shooters, who wore revealing outfits or bragged about their sharp eye and mistake-free shooting, Annie was a modest girl no taller than five feet and of small build. She appeared as a child to any viewer in the audience, which made her shooting act even more amazing. Annie also dressed modestly, wearing a black dress with cuffed sleeves and a white collar. Her looks and her attitude made her even more appealing to the audience, as she always wore a wide smile on her face, which was framed with her long dark hair.

Phoebe Ann Moses was a true definition of a rising star, and her stage name of "Annie Oakley" seemed to carry a note of magic itself, as it was melodic and easy for the audience to remember. Annie never revealed why she picked that name. As time passed, people were curious about the origins of this unparalleled sharpshooter. While some have suggested Annie took the name "Oakley" based on the neighborhood in which she and Butler resided, others have suggested that it was the name of the man who paid her train fare when she was running away from the "wolves."

What is known is that Annie disliked her family name, Moses, insisting that her family's name was actually "Mozey." She even entered a feud with her brother when she had the name "Mozey" engraved on the headstones of her two nephews who had died.

Whatever the reason for picking her stage name, Annie created a brand and was easily recognizable as one of the top sharpshooting performers of her time. However, very little is known about the first year of Annie and Butler working together. It is presumed they mostly performed in the Great Lakes region and the Midwest during 1883.

Working alongside Butler involved a lot of traveling, which wasn't unusual for performers and even famous actors at the time. Annie and Frank Butler mostly depended on trains, boardinghouses, and cheap hotels to save some money. As Annie said on one occasion, saving money on traveling meant that she could afford pretty hair ribbons, nice new gloves, and other things she would wear to look neat and pretty for the show. She never relied on her sexuality to earn money and attract more spectators. She looked like a plain but interesting and attractive woman, who could rely on her charming smile and her undisputed sharpshooting skills to win over the audience.

Frank was the perfect partner for Annie, as he loved and cherished her for who she was. He never took credit for her skill, saying that he couldn't have taught her to shoot since she could outshoot him even before she became a performer. He said the only thing he did for Annie's career was to get her a position as his partner.

As Annie's popularity grew, Frank allowed her to have the entire show to herself, and he settled into the role of manager. Frank made sure to manage Annie's bookings, talk to theater managers, check the train schedules, count and keep their earnings, and place ads in newspapers to advertise Annie's sharpshooting shows.

Annie was more than happy with how Frank managed her bookings and their finances, on one occasion saying that she had whatever she owned due to Frank's "careful management." Annie and Frank were still poor when they started doing shows together. When Annie was just starting out as the main star of the show, they had enough money to buy her a pretty hat after a week's work.

Soon, they were tired of counting every penny they earned, as they were constantly going through financial struggles, so the pair decided to join the Sells Brothers, who offered them a contract for forty weeks. With the Sells Brothers Circus, Annie and Frank wouldn't have to worry about traveling fares and paychecks, as they would get fair compensation for their performance and could save up some money while performing a couple of times a day.

However, before Annie Oakley and Frank Butler joined the Sells brothers, Annie performed in the Olympic Theater in St. Paul, Minnesota. It was a show that would become known as one of the most memorable moments in the life and work of Annie Oakley, as it was when she became known as "Little Sure Shot."

Chapter 5 – Miss "Little Sure Shot" and Chief Sitting Bull

Back in March of 1884, Annie was still struggling to get the recognition she thought she deserved. Frank and Annie wanted to get all the bookings they could during that winter, so they accepted a job to join a traveling show known as the Arlington and Fields Combination.

Annie grew up in poverty, and she was driven to achieve financial stability and enjoy the fruits of her labor and efforts. Annie competed in shooting matches during the day and performed in the evenings. She was too busy to notice what was going on in St. Paul the week the traveling show arrived in that town.

What Annie didn't know at the time when she and Frank arrived in St. Paul was that one of the most infamous prisoners of the Territory of Dakota was in town as well. Chief Sitting Bull of the Hunkpapa Lakota was visiting St. Paul. He was blamed for the death of Lieutenant Colonel George Armstrong Custer in the Battle of the Little Bighorn, which took place eight years before.

While Sitting Bull did not directly partake in the fighting, he was an easy scapegoat, as he was the leader of the rebels who defeated Custer. The American forces were brutally defeated in this battle, which stands as one of the most significant actions of the Great Sioux War. For that reason, Chief Sitting Bull was hated amongst the people of St. Paul, as well as many other places. In March 1884, Chief Sitting Bull, who, after surrendering to authorities in 1881, lived at the Standing Rock Agency near Fort Yates, arrived in St. Paul with Indian Agent James McLaughlin.

Agent McLaughlin had brought Sitting Bull and his nephew One Bull to tour various parts of the country. In St. Paul, they visited schools, a cigar factory, where Sitting Bull rolled a cigar and then smoked it, and a millinery, where they were greeted by forty women who worked there.

Sioux Chief Sitting Bull, 1885. The United States Library of Congress Prints and Photographs Division

https://commons.wikimedia.org/wiki/File:Sitting_Bull_by_D_F_Barry_ca_1883_Dakota_Territory.jpg

The women from the millinery decorated the Sioux chief's hair with ribbons, which made Sitting Bull appear far less ferocious to the locals of St. Paul. Although many feared Sitting Bull and even resented him for his conflicts with the US Army, there was something admirable about the chief. He always looked people in the eye while talking to them, and he always spoke clearly and deliberately.

At night, after taking a tour around the town, Sitting Bull went to the theater. On the first night of his visit, the chief enjoyed "Muldoon's Picnic" at the Grand Opera House, and the next night, he laughed at the Dr. Reed show. On the third evening, Chief Sitting Bull was taken to see the Arlington and Fields Combination show at the Olympic Theater.

At the time, Arlington and Fields Combination advertised their shows as the greatest congregation of talent ever to arrive at St. Paul. The chief enjoyed the acrobatics show, the singing of Miss Allie Jackson, and watched the afterpiece called "St. Patrick's Day in the Evening." A part of the show included Annie Oakley's shooting exhibition.

Frank assisted Annie as she shot cigarettes off his lips, corks off bottles with unearthly precision, and blew out the flames of candles with bullets flying by. Chief Sitting Bull observed Annie's act in awe. He was so fascinated by the petite girl with long dark hair, blue eyes, and steady hand and eye that he decided to meet Annie Oakley in person.

Annie Oakley, Underwood Archives

The same night after the show, as well as days afterward, Chief Sitting Bull sent his messengers to Annie, asking to meet her in person. Annie and Frank were staying at the hotel in St. Paul, and Annie's mind was only set on work and money. Since she competed in shooting matches during the day, she didn't have time to meet Chief Sitting Bull. But the chief didn't give up. He kept sending his messengers in hopes of meeting Annie.

The chief must have eventually realized that Annie cared more about earning money and that she couldn't spare the time to meet him because of her busy working schedule, as he decided to send her sixty-five dollars along with a message saying he would like to have a photograph of her as a memory of her talent and unique and charming appearance.

Annie was so amused by the chief's decisiveness to meet her that she decided to accept the invitation. She returned the message, agreeing to meet the chief and also returning the money he had sent. After meeting Annie Oakley in person, Sitting Bull was so taken with her that he wanted to adopt her, giving her the name "Watanya Cicilla," which translates to "Little Sure Shot." Thus, Annie symbolically became a daughter of a chieftain, which came with certain privileges that Oakley liked to brag about. Annie liked to talk about how she was entitled to have five ponies, an endless number of cattle, other presents in livestock, and a wigwam.

Frank made the business decision to utilize the story of the adoption as an advertisement for Annie's show. Frank made a publication in the *New York Clipper*, advertising Annie through the prism of Sitting Bull's fascination. As proof of the chief's admiration, Annie had the original moccasins the chief wore, a feather from his hair, and a photograph of him, which was given to her as a present.

What Annie might not have noticed was that the chief might have had a romantic interest in her, even though most believe his interest was more fatherly in nature.

With this move, Annie became known as "the greatest of the greatest" and the main star of "the best shooting show ever seen," as advertised by Frank and promoted through the famous Chief Sitting Bull.

The legend of Annie Oakley, Little Miss Sure Shot, was born. However, it would take some time until Annie became a major star in the world of Wild West entertainment.

Chapter 6 – A Faithful Trip to New Orleans: Buffalo Bill's Wild West Show

Frank and Annie worked on a variety of shows for the Sells Brothers Circus. However, they didn't make enough money to live solely off their shooting acts in the circus, so Annie and Frank participated in a comic act as well. In addition, Annie rode a side-saddle for the Rose Garland entrée. If anything, the Sells brothers knew how to make a show and attract a crowd.

They arrived in New Orleans with fifty wild animals, which included a pair of hippopotamuses, a grown giraffe, and an arsenal of wild beasts, birds, and even an aquarium of amphibious sea creatures. The circus also introduced Chemah, a Chinese dwarf, who was advertised as the tiniest man on earth. Annie and Frank were certainly earning their dime with the contract they had with the Sells brothers.

Although the pair performed for thousands of people across 187 cities in 18 states, the name of Annie Oakley and Frank Butler barely made it to the newspapers. An elephant named Emperor, which was a part of the Sells Brothers Circus, received more fame at the time than the sharpshooting duo.

In late 1884, during the World Industrial and Cotton Centennial Exposition, all of New Orleans was decorated with flowers, as the city was celebrating a hundred years since America started to export cotton. Exhibitions were set up, and every country brought its own variety of plants, with Texas alone bringing over 21,000 different specimens. The Sells Brothers wanted to cash in on the crowds arriving in New Orleans. That day, there were over 25,000 people on the streets, all renting rooms in hotels and all looking for something to do as they waited for the exhibition to open.

The Sells Brothers Circus had a fair number of visitors, but the number wasn't as high as the brothers would have liked, as it was constantly raining. The Sells brothers had planned to stay in New Orleans for the exhibition opening, but the stubborn and persistent rain changed their minds. After only two weeks, the brothers decided to close and head home.

Annie and Frank still had a contract with the Sells brothers, and they renewed their contract for the next season. The next season, though, wouldn't start until April. Even though there was an increase in salary, the sharpshooting duo was left without a job in December 1884 while staying in New Orleans, Louisiana. They had four months before the start of their new contract, which meant they had to find a way to make some money until the next circus season started.

Frank started to look for work and bookings for their show. As he often used to do, Frank listed an advertisement in a trade publication known as the *Clipper*, hoping to hear from a prominent employer.

Frank was a keen reader of newspapers, and only several days after publishing the advertisement, he stumbled upon an ad that caught his interest. It read, "Mr. E. W. Woodcott, Buffalo Bill's Wild West show—an original American amusement enterprise."

Woodcott was the general manager for Buffalo Bill's Wild West show, which contained a great number of shooting acts and horse racing. To Frank, the fact Buffalo Bill's show was arriving in New Orleans was a sign that he and Annie should stay in New Orleans and try to score a shooting act. The prominent William Frederick Cody, better known as Buffalo Bill, arrived in New Orleans on December 8th, 1884, and the Sells Brothers Circus left the city only several days later, on December 13th.

Buffalo Bill's Wild West show poster

Before the Sells Brothers Circus departed, Buffalo Bill paid for a ticket to see one of their shows. On that occasion, he asked to meet Annie Oakley and Frank Butler. The pair saw this as the perfect opportunity to ask for a job at his Wild West show; however, they were turned down by Buffalo Bill, who said the show already had more than enough shooting acts.

Recalling this event in her autobiography, Annie said that her vanity was wounded, but she saw consolation in the fact that one of the shooters performing for the Wild West show was the famous Captain Adam Bogardus. Bogardus performed with his sons, Peter, Henry, Edward, and Eugene, and he was also a part-owner of Buffalo Bill's Wild West show.

For Annie and Frank, Buffalo Bill's refusal meant they had no further business in New Orleans, and not wanting to spend their winter in idleness, they packed their bags and headed north, performing in a variety of shows. Buffalo Bill's show moved on without them, opening acts in New Orleans that winter of 1884.

Buffalo Bill had a tough season that year, and his troubles began with the transportation of equipment and animals for the show. The steamship that was transporting the show collided with a steamboat on the Mississippi River, and the show's equipment sank. The losses included guns, ammunition, wagons, camp equipment, and animals. The losses were so great that Bogardus decided to head to Cincinnati to try and find the owner of the steamboat and recoup the damages done to their equipment and the steamer.

The weather wasn't in their favor either, as it was constantly raining, and Cody had to postpone the start of the season in New Orleans more than several times. In March 1885, Bogardus was so fed up with their bad luck that he announced he was going back home and was taking his sons with him. Bogardus planned to enroll his sons back in school. This was yet another blow to Buffalo Bill, as he had now lost the greatest stars of his shooting acts, Bogardus and his four sons.

However, one man's misfortune is often another man's luck. Annie and Frank saw a new opportunity once they heard of Bogardus's departure. Annie immediately wrote to Cody, asking for a place in the show for Frank and herself. However, Annie wanted a fairly high salary, and Buffalo Bill was already in debt for an estimated $60,000 due to the horrible winter the show had in New Orleans. Cody responded to Annie, claiming that her payment demands were rather steep. He was also worried that such a small woman wasn't fit to take over the act that had been previously led by Bogardus and his sons. Each of Bogardus's rifles weighed at least ten pounds, and Cody didn't think a woman of barely 110 pounds could carry, shoot, and use these guns day after day.

Buffalo Bill shared his concerns with Annie, suggesting that she wouldn't be able to withstand the recoil from these guns. Annie Oakley's confidence was so great that she wasn't ready to back down, but she asked for a thirty-day trial during which she could prove her ability to perform. If she wasn't up to the task, Annie promised to leave the show as soon as the trial expired. Cody agreed, and Annie and Frank planned to meet up with the show in Louisville, Kentucky, where the show was supposed to open in the last week of April.

Before Annie and Frank headed to Louisville, Annie wanted to practice her shooting stunts in the same manner as Bogardus and Doc Carver. Annie decided to use three 16-gauge Parker shotguns to shoot 5,000 glass balls in a single day. However, Annie was up for the challenge, as she shot 4,772 glass balls in nine hours, finishing the endurance test by shooting an additional 984 glass balls. She announced this shooting feat as her personal record. Annie was determined to make a name for herself and join Buffalo Bill's Wild West show.

Many historians wonder why Oakley and Butler wanted to join the Wild West show so badly, especially since the show was already in debt and had suffered a difficult year, losing property, money, and the star of their shooting exhibitions, Bogardus. However, it was more than obvious that Annie was growing tired of variety shows, as there were too many shooters to compete with. It was becoming difficult to make a living and save money with so many sharpshooters constantly raising the bar. Moreover, by 1884, there were so many shooting acts that Annie lost her edge as being a woman shooter. Frank heard of at least twenty women doing the same thing, some of which used tricks to make the audience believe their hand was as steady as Annie's was.

Annie and Frank had never heard of a female shooter using a shotgun, though, so they decided to grab the opportunity and use it the best they could. Annie Oakley was ready to join Buffalo Bill's Wild West show, which was known at the time as the greatest outdoor show in America.

Chapter 7 – "The Greatest Entertainment Show in American History"

It wasn't vanity that drove Buffalo's Bill Wild West show to be known as the greatest entertainment show in American history. William F. Cody, a.k.a. Buffalo Bill, became a legend after working thirteen years in show business. He made sure that everyone in America and Europe had heard of his show. The successful combination of rodeo drama skits, which promoted and romanticized the way of life in the Wild West, and marksmanship shows and shooting exhibitions made his show incredibly popular. However, they weren't the only things that attracted people enough to pay fifty cents. People also came to see the legendary folk hero Buffalo Bill himself, who was just as charming and awing in his appearance as he was in his reputation. Cody was a heavy-drinking man, but he was still friendly and approachable. He had a long dark goatee and long dark hair, and he had a talent for putting on a show.

A cowboy band would play at the opening of the Wild West shows, and Buffalo Bill would introduce himself alongside Native American horse riders, who shouted and chanted while the bells on their horses' necks jangled as they sprinted around the stage. Cowboys and Mexican vaqueros would join Cody and the Native American riders on the stage, and Cody would give them a sign by shouting out. Once the riders were given the sign, they would start letting out war whoops, and their colorful feathers swirled in a dizzying display, intertwining paths with the Mexican vaqueros and cowboys. Shots would be fired into the air as the riders shouted and circled the stage. This kind of opening fired the audience up, setting a high level of energy right from the get-go.

When Annie and Frank arrived in Kentucky, where the Wild West show would open for the season, Cody was nowhere to be found. The duo was told that Buffalo Bill was out parading the streets with other members of the troop. Annie and Frank decided to unload their guns, bags, and other equipment so Annie could get some practice in before Cody returned to the camp.

Frank and Annie brought a big load of guns into the arena. They noticed that a man was sitting there, who barely even acknowledged their presence. Annie picked up her shotgun and started to shot clay pigeons in the arena.

The man who was observing Annie's practice didn't look like a part of the Wild West show, as he wore fancy clothes and carried a slim ornate cane, but as soon as Annie finished shooting, he got up without hesitation to tell her how impressed he was with her marksmanship skills.

As it turned out, the man was the business manager of the Wild West show, Nate Salsbury. Salsbury decided to hire Annie and neglect the thirty-day trial period without even consulting Cody, remarking that a woman with Annie's skill, shooting targets with a shotgun, was a novelty in shooting shows.

MISS ANNIE OAKLEY,
THE PEERLESS LADY WING-SHOT.

Annie Oakley in a Buffalo Bill's Wild West show poster

Annie wrote in her autobiography that Salsbury ordered posters to advertise Annie's act, as well as woodcarving of her, which cost him around $7,000. Annie found this odd, as she knew that someone who hadn't firmly established themselves in the industry shouldn't be advertised in such a vigorous way. Annie was later told that Salsbury talked about her with Cody, using only words of praise to describe her and calling her a "real daisy." According to Salsbury, Annie Oakley was an exceptional talent, and she would give the Wild West show an opportunity to offer a novelty to amusement-hungry audiences across America.

Soon, Annie and Frank met up with Cody. Buffalo Bill started to call Annie Oakley "Annie Missi," which was a nickname that soon stuck, although only people who were close to her could call her by that name. The name "Missi" was a clever combination of "Mississippi" and "Missy." Annie would call Cody "the Colonel." Later on, Annie described Cody as the kindest man with the biggest heart, a man who was loyal, simple, and trustworthy. Annie said in her autobiography that the Colonel had honest relationships with everyone he encountered and that he was the most trusting man she had ever met.

Annie and Frank were welcomed to the Buffalo Bill's Wild West show family. It was the first time Annie faced the real Wild West and met real cowboys. The show consisted of cowboys, Native American riders, who mostly hailed from the Sioux, and Mexican vaqueros; Annie was the first white woman to join the largest and greatest Wild West show in America. She would soon become one of the most popular Wild West characters, even though she had never been a part of that world and never concealed the fact that she came from Ohio.

Annie secured herself a solo act for Buffalo Bill's Wild West show, where she would remain for the next seventeen years.

Chapter 8 – Annie Oakley as the Heart of the Wild West Show

Annie Oakley was finally at the point where she could say that people knew her name, and it was all thanks to her skills, talent, her husband's management, and her determination to get herself an act in Buffalo Bill's Wild West show.

Her act was simple but charming. It only lasted about ten minutes, but ten minutes was more than enough time to enchant the audience and become the heart of the Wild West show.

Annie would enter the stage, waving to the audience and sending kisses. She looked like an innocent, charming girl. She wore a short skirt that fell below her knees and a shirt that was loose around her waist so she could use her full motion potential. She even used a skill she had learned years back at the Darke County Infirmary and sewed flowers and ribbons on her skirts. Even though she stood out with her looks and appearance from the rest of the Wild West show, Annie still wore a wide-edged sombrero with a six-pointed star attached to it, showcasing her attachment to the show.

People who worked with Annie told stories about how she was a neat woman that took great care and pride in her outfits and the way she dressed. She always wanted everything to be perfect, so her clothes had to be sewn to perfection as well.

At the beginning of her act, Annie ran to the center of the shooting arena, where she would meet Frank, who stood there without the introduction Annie Oakley would receive as the star of the show. Annie then unveiled a table with weapons, while Frank prepared to assist her in the act.

After picking up a shotgun, Annie would shoot at the clay pigeons Frank threw in the air. He raised the excitement and difficulty of Annie's challenge by adding more pigeons to his pitches. Annie would hit all of the targets. Even if she happened to miss the first time, she always got it the second time.

Annie was swift and fast, shooting with a steady arm and a steady eye. However, she wasn't only quick; she could also use both hands to shoot since she was ambidextrous. She would take two guns and shoot at the targets simultaneously, putting on a real show for the excited crowd.

Moving around the arena and shooting from almost any imaginable position and angle, Annie showed that a woman could be as equally agile and athletic as men. She would take a glass ball and throw it herself, shooting it on the first try in a blink of an eye.

One of the audience's most favorite acts was Annie's shooting stunt that used a mirror or a polished kitchen knife. She used the mirror to observe the target behind her back and shot the gun over her shoulder. Another popular stunt involved Annie's swiftness, as well as her athletic and marksmanship skills. Annie would lay her shotgun on the ground and stand ten feet away in the opposite direction. Frank, who was standing opposite Annie and the gun, would throw a clay pigeon in the air, and Annie would run toward the shotgun and shoot the clay pigeon before it touched the ground.

Annie's most difficult and challenging task was performed at the end of her act. It included eleven glass balls, five shotguns, and a single rifle. Annie had only ten seconds to shoot eleven balls while switching between the rifle and five shotguns. This exhibition was described by the press as "the cleverest number." At the end of her ten-minute show, Annie Oakley would run across the stage, sending kisses to the audience yet again. Just before she left the stage, she would make a little kick.

Annie wasn't only a sharpshooter—she was also a performer. She knew how to engage the audience and make them laugh. If she missed the target, she would stomp her feet as if she was upset, giving off the impression of a little girl throwing a tantrum, which was enough to charm the audience.

Comedy was an important part of Annie Oakley's show. On one occasion, Annie kept missing her targets, clay pigeons in this case, so she acted all upset and took Frank's hat. She threw it in the air and then shot straight through it on the first try.

Annie Oakley shooting over her shoulder in the famous mirror stunt

At times when she missed her targets, she amused her audience by laying her shotgun on the ground and walking around it, as superstitious shooters walk around their guns and rifles to change their luck. Annie wasn't superstitious at all, though; she was just doing it to amuse the audience. After walking around her shotgun for some time, Annie would pick it up, and Frank would start throwing clay pigeons again, with Annie hitting all the targets.

Annie's shooting skills and her comedic performance brought her fame. Her name became more popular across America every day. Annie was excellent at what she did, and it must have been an incredible sight to watch her shoot targets and perform stunts.

Annie was so swift, and her aim was so good that many implied that she somehow cheated when it came to her shooting stunts. Cheating in shooting shows wasn't a rare occurrence. Many sharpshooters cheated, as they focused more on amusing and awing the audience than on practicing their shooting. It also didn't help that Annie was living in a man's world, as many most likely wouldn't know a woman could be that good.

However, Annie and Frank knew the ways of the entertainment business. Frank knew that Annie was talented enough not to miss her targets, but when she made it look easy, people questioned the authenticity of her marksmanship. The two agreed that Annie should occasionally miss a target or two, which would prove that she was not a cheater since she didn't hit every target flawlessly.

In many ways, Annie was the heart of the Wild West show. Not only did the audience adore her, but Cody himself and the rest of the troop also respected Annie's feelings and her straightforward persona.

Annie never liked to be called a champion of sharpshooting, as she feared she might become associated with fakes and immoral shooters. Regardless, she cared much for her reputation. When the troop became intoxicated or had inappropriate company around, she would ask them to avoid her. The troop respected her wishes, and they also avoided cursing, smoking, and drinking in front of her. Annie never smoked, heavily drank, or cursed, although she did enjoy an occasional beer. However, she would never pay for one herself; Annie only drank if someone offered her a cold one.

Chapter 9 – Rivalry, Royals, and Rifles

During her long career at Buffalo Bill's Wild West show, Annie met new friends and reencountered old ones while also finding foes and rivals.

Sitting Bull joined Buffalo Bill's Wild West show soon after Annie Oakley did. Even though legend implies the chief agreed to join the show because Annie Oakley was a part of the troop, Sitting Bull was actually convinced to sign up because he was promised a fair salary, bonuses, and exclusive right to sell his autographed photos to admirers.

John Burke, who was the chief promoter for Buffalo Bill's Wild West show, was happy Sitting Bull would become a part of the show. Burke had tried to convince Sitting Bull to join the show on several occasions but with no success. Although Sitting Bull didn't join because Annie was a part of the troop, he was, nonetheless, thrilled to see her as one of the show's performers. Although Annie Oakley and Sitting Bull had a prior relationship, with Sitting Bull symbolically adopting Annie as his daughter, Burke never utilized their acquaintance and the story of Annie's adoption to advertise their acts.

The two actually never shared the stage, as they performed in individual acts.

Annie Oakley became a respected and loved character on stage, as well as backstage, but a particular rivalry was brought center stage a year later in 1886. Young Lillian Smith, whose fame somewhat didn't outlive her the way it has with Annie Oakley, was only fifteen years old when she signed a contract with Buffalo Bill. Lillian Smith had been shooting since the age of seven, and she was eleven years younger than Annie. Even though the two female sharpshooters weren't advertised as rivals, the audience surely judged them by this important rivalry.

Annie Oakley still stood proudly and put all her energy into her acts, although she chipped six years off her real age once Lillian joined the Wild West show. Lillian, as a promising fifteen-year-old shooter, was advertised by Buffalo Bill as the "Californian huntress." She was poised to become the next rising star of sharpshooting.

Lillian and Annie were what could be called radical opposites, although the two were nearly equal when it came to their sharpshooting skills. Most likely because Lillian was younger than

Annie Oakley, she was full of confidence and liked to brag. Annie recalled hearing Lillian say upon her arrival that "Annie Oakley was done for." Lillian would wear flashy clothes, which was very different from Annie's neat and simple skirts. Annie Oakley was also modest when it came to her achievements, as she always refused to be called a champion. The two even used different weapons for their shooting exhibitions, with Lillian favoring a rifle and Annie a shotgun.

One thing was certain—Annie Oakley wasn't the only girl in the troop, and the audience loved fantasizing about the rivalry between the two female performers. Even though Annie didn't seem to care much about the alleged rivalry and the fact that Lillian often boasted about her skill and how she could beat Annie at any time, the tension between the two still rose, hitting its peak a year later.

In 1887, Buffalo Bill's Wild West show headed to London, England, where Queen Victoria, Prince Edward, and the royal family were supposed to attend the show. Shooting matches were also organized at Wimbledon, and both Annie Oakley and Lillian Smith planned to show off their shooting skills at the event.

By the time the Wild West show arrived in London, Annie's name was already famous, which meant the queen didn't miss a chance to praise Annie Oakley for her talent and reputation, as well as to shake her hand. Lillian Smith was neglected in a way and remained in the shadow of Annie, although she was welcomed appropriately by the royals.

The British press mostly covered the story about Annie meeting the queen, sharing the news that Queen Victoria had only words of praise for Annie Oakley. However, the American press seemed to have liked the idea of having a top sharpshooter such as Annie being in the shadow of a younger shooter, Lillian Smith. American newspapers reported that Lillian was welcomed with praises while Annie Oakley remained on the sidelines.

While Lillian was given all the publicity that she could have asked for, which was helped by the support of Buffalo Bill, the publicity stunt failed once Annie and Lillian competed at Wimbledon. Even before the match, some Americans suggested that Lillian wasn't a match for Annie's skill and that the young shooter was a trickster. However, for Colonel Cody, having Lillian as a part of the troop was a huge win for the Wild West show. Thus, Cody refused to comment on the news that favored Lillian and bashed Annie's importance. Annie still respected Cody even though he didn't stand up for her.

However, the truth about the skill of both sharpshooters emerged several days after the ricochet of offenses on Annie's reputation. Lillian performed poorly at Wimbledon, destroying her chance to show that she was better than Annie. Annie, on the other hand, showcased her skill in all its glory, proving that she was the actual champion of sharpshooting, even though she never favored that title. Annie Oakley was so brilliant in her performance at Wimbledon that Prince Edward himself left his seat to shake hands with the sharpshooting legend.

Despite this, Buffalo Bill still favored young Lillian Smith. It was probably due to this that Annie decided to leave Buffalo Bill's Wild West show.

However, the story of Annie Oakley isn't over yet.

Chapter 10 – The Aftermath and Well-deserved Glory

Annie Oakley and Frank Butler left Buffalo Bill's Wild West show in 1888, after which Annie joined a rivaling Wild West show. She also joined the theater and got back to performing on stage, even acting in a play called *Deadwood Dick*. In between, Annie Oakley participated in shooting matches across Philadelphia. Idleness just wasn't an option for Annie and Frank, so they kept doing what they did best.

Annie Oakley wasn't away from Buffalo Bill and his crew for long, as she decided to return once Lillian Smith left the show in 1889. Lillian later reinvented herself at an older age, performing as an "Indian princess"; however, she was never immortalized in folklore the way Annie Oakley has been.

Annie returned to Buffalo Bill's show just in time to take off for a tour in Europe, which commenced with the Paris Exposition. The Eiffel Tower was a novelty at the time, as it had just been built, and France was celebrating its centennial anniversary of the French Revolution. The exposition was visited by roughly thirty-two million people from around the world. Annie's performance was so brilliant that the president of France told her she could join the French Army for a commission. At the same time, the king of Senegal offered

Annie Oakley $100,000 to help him get rid of the tigers plaguing his country. Annie refused these offers. Annie also met Thomas Edison and asked him if he would be able to make an electric gun. Edison told Annie he would consider her idea, and Annie refused offers that she received from the President of France and the King of Senegal.

The tour in Paris lasted for six months, and after that, the Wild West show embarked on a three-year tour around Europe. Buffalo Bill's troop returned to America in October 1892 to find that the United States Census Bureau had declared an end to the American frontier since settlements were now widespread.

During the Wild West show tour in Europe in 1890, Annie Oakley visited Berlin. The last German Kaiser, Friedrich Wilhelm II, was in attendance. The Kaiser was a great admirer of Annie Oakley and had already viewed a few of her shows. As an exhibition shooter, Annie used to include all sorts of stunts in her act, and one of these stunts included asking for a volunteer who would agree to become a part of a rather dangerous act.

Annie asked if anyone from the audience wanted to volunteer to hold a cigarette in his mouth while Annie attempted to shoot the ashes clean off. No one would ever volunteer, so Frank would join Annie on the stage for the stunt. However, it was different at the Berlin show, as there was a volunteer—the German Kaiser himself.

Annie had no other options, knowing that she could not refuse one of the most powerful men in the world, so she invited him to join her on stage. The Kaiser's life was in Annie's hands as she raised her rifle. The Kaiser lit a cigarette, placed it in his mouth, and waited for Annie's shot. Annie pulled the trigger and shot the ashes right off the Kaiser's cigarette without any problem.

After performing in many successful tours, Annie Oakley was rather famous, and her every word was carefully monitored by the media and public. Her interviews could be found in practically every newspaper, and everyone wanted to meet her.

In May 1893, Annie and the rest of the troop joined the Chicago Columbia Exposition, which celebrated the 400th anniversary of Columbus arriving in the Americas. This year was the best for the Wild West show by far, as around six million people visited the show during the exposition. The show made about one million dollars that season.

The same year, Frank and Annie bought a new home in Nutley, New Jersey, where they moved in after the season ended. During the summer of 1894, Annie joined the Wild West show in Brooklyn, where they were able to perform at night for the first time since the show now owned a massive array of electric lights. In the fall of the same year, Annie Oakley traveled to meet Thomas Edison, who wanted to test a kinetoscope, a harbinger of the motion picture camera. Thomas Edison wanted to see if the kinetoscope could capture the smoke from Annie's gun, which it did. In October, the Wild West show ended its season to Cody's dissatisfaction, as the show didn't earn much. Colonel Cody blamed the cost of running electric lights and the ongoing economic depression for the lack of profit that year.

The next year, in 1895, Cody had a plan to earn enough to make up for the lack of profit from the last season, so the Wild West show embarked on another tour across America, visiting 131 cities. According to Annie's estimates, she fired around 40,000 bullets in a year.

In 1900, Annie performed for the first time with the Wild West show in Greenville, her hometown. The townspeople presented her with a commemorative silver cup, which Annie stated was the dearest award she had ever received. The next year, in 1901, just as the season with the show was ending, Frank and Annie ended up in a train accident. A show train carrying Buffalo Bill's troop was hit by a fast southbound train. The accident occurred near Lexington, and the collision derailed Annie Oakley's private car, which was attached to the train. At the time, the newspapers didn't write about Annie being injured. However, Frank had to take her to the hospital, where she was diagnosed with internal injuries, and her left side was temporarily paralyzed. The doctor thought that Annie would never shoot again.

The train accident left many people injured, and 110 horses owned by Buffalo Bill ended up either dead or had to be put down due to injuries. Two of the horses that died had been given to Buffalo Bill by the queen of England as a present. Supposedly, Buffalo Bill cried once he discovered his horses had died.

Annie decided that she couldn't travel with the show any longer. She quit the next year, and Frank accepted a job as a representative for the Union Metallic Cartridge Company.

Annie returned to the stage in 1902, starring in *The Western Girl*, which was another success for her. However, the next year, despite her success, the name of Annie Oakley was intentionally stained by journalist William Randolph Hearst. Hearst published sensational and popular stories, and he wrote that Annie Oakley was in prison for stealing a pair of pants from "a negro" to buy cocaine and soothe her drug addiction. The news was read from coast to coast, and although it was untrue, everyone was talking about the scandal.

Annie cherished her reputation, so she decided to file fifty-five lawsuits to get to the bottom of the false news and make things right. The legal battle would last until 1910, with Oakley traveling to various courts across the country to testify. In the meantime, Hearst wanted to smear Oakley's reputation even further and hired a private detective, sending him to Greenville to dig up dirt on America's favorite sharpshooter.

There was nothing to be found, of course, as Annie was an honorable girl who didn't use drugs or imbibe alcohol. She won fifty-four out of the fifty-five lawsuits and collected around $27,500. The entire amount was spent on court expenses.

During her career as a sharpshooter, Annie never missed a chance to pay a visit to her mother. In August 1908, Annie found out that her mother had died, and she immediately returned to Ohio.

Two years later, in 1910, Annie paid a visit to Buffalo Bill's Wild West show, and Colonel Cody asked her to return. Annie declined and joined a rivaling show called Young Buffalo Wild West in 1911. She performed with the show for two years and traveled across the country, even though she was already fifty years old. In 1913, Annie decided that her career as a performer had come to an end and quit performing in shows.

Frank and Annie moved into a waterfront cottage in Maryland, near Cambridge. In the meantime, Colonel Cody's show went bankrupt, and the Wild West show memorabilia was sold by creditors.

In the summer of 1915, Annie and Frank decide to visit Cody, whose health was declining. The pair then decided to spend a winter in Pinehurst, North Carolina. Annie decided to give lessons to girls who wanted to learn how to shoot. It is believed that throughout her life, Annie taught over 15,000 women how to handle a gun. Sadly, Cody never got better. He died in 1917, and although Annie couldn't attend his funeral, she wrote a eulogy for him that ran in all the newspapers across America. She described Cody as the kindest and most lovable man she had ever met.

The same year, the United States entered the First World War, and Annie telegraphed the war secretary to offer her services in recruiting a regiment of female shooters to help America win the war. She never got a reply, and the regiment was never compiled. Instead, Annie organized shooting demonstrations to raise money at army camps across the country.

The next year, the Allies won the war, and Annie joined the celebration. Four years later, in 1922, Annie joined a charity event on Long Island to help collect money for wounded soldiers. Although she was already sixty-two years old, Annie could still shoot like the legend she had been all her life. However, this was one of the last times she would shoot a firearm.

Annie Oakley, 1922. New York World-Telegram & Sun Collection

That November, Annie had a car accident, and she injured her hip and ankle. She would wear a leg brace for the rest of her life. After the accident, Annie stopped shooting for good. In 1924, Frank and Annie moved to Dayton, Ohio. In 1926, Oakley's health began to decline sharply, and Frank and Annie decided to move to Greenville, where Annie died on November 3rd, 1926, only months after moving back. Frank and Annie had been married for fifty years. According to some sources, his love for Annie was so great that he stopped eating and died of starvation eighteen days after Annie passed.

The story of one of America's greatest sharpshooters ended where it had started, in Darke County, with a man who adored her since the day they met.

Less than ten years after her death, the first story about Annie Oakley's life emerged on the big screens. The movie was followed by a musical in 1946 called *Annie Get Your Gun*, with lyrics and music by Irving Berlin. The Broadway show was later made into a film and a TV show, and the musical has been revived numerous times since its initial run.

Conclusion

The American frontier gave birth to dazzling shooting shows and romanticized life in the Wild West. In such a world, there was hardly any place for a woman. However, Annie Oakley managed to make a name for herself and became nothing less than one of the most famous figures on the sharpshooting scene. Although she was not born on the frontier, Annie became a legend herself, and she is immortalized even a century later as one of the best female shooters the world has ever seen.

During her fifty-year-long career, Annie dazzled and awed various audiences around Europe and America and became a symbol of the Wild West. Not only did she win the hearts of people with her shooting skill and talent, but she also stole attention with her unique appearance and flawless sense for performance and comedy.

Due to her steady hand and steady eye, Annie Oakley will most likely always be remembered as one of the greatest, and perhaps unsuspected, folklore heroines of the Wild West.

Here's another book by Captivating History that you might like

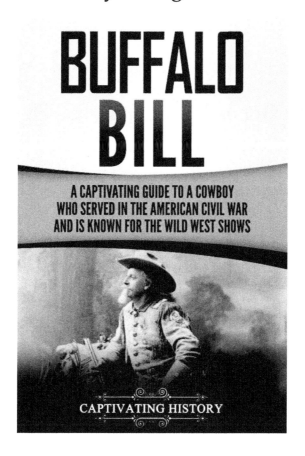

Free Bonus from Captivating History (Available for a Limited time)

Hi History Lovers!

Now you have a chance to join our exclusive history list so you can get your first history ebook for free as well as discounts and a potential to get more history books for free! Simply visit the link below to join.

Captivatinghistory.com/ebook

Also, make sure to follow us on Facebook, Twitter and Youtube by searching for Captivating History.

References

1. "Annie Oakley." lkwdpl.org Women in History. Archived from the original on July 13, 2012. Accessed in November 2020.

2. Haugen, B., *Annie Oakley: American Sharpshooter*, Capstone, 2006, p. 88.

3. "Annie Oakley." Dorchester County Public Library, Cambridge, MD. Archived from the original on February 22, 2008. Retrieved January 20, 2007. Accessed in November 2020.

4. *"Little Sure Shot" The Saga of Annie Oakley*, Caroline Kim-Brown. 2006.

5. *The Life and Legacy of Annie Oakley, Volume Seven*, The Oklahoma Western Biographies, Glenda Riley, 2002.

6. *Annie Oakley*, Shirl Kasper, 2000.

7. *Annie Oakley of the Wild West*, Walter Havighurst, 2003.

Printed in Great Britain
by Amazon